Voyager Passport F

Fluency 6

ISBN 978-1-4168-0670-7

Copyright 2008 by Voyager Expanded Learning, L.P.

All rights reserved. No part of this publication may be reproduced or transmitted in any form or by any means, electronic or mechanical, including photocopy, recording, or any information storage and retrieval system, without permission in writing from the publisher.

Printed in the United States of America   08 09 10 11 12 13   DIG   9 8 7 6 5 4 3 2

Table of Contents

Signs and Symbols

Symbols on the Dollar Bill 1

Too Many Red Things 2

A Visit to the Vietnam Memorial 3

Looking at Maps 4

The Bald Eagle 5

Exciting Games

Family from Lee County Enjoys New Sport 6

Climbing Walls of Rock 7

If at First You Don't Succeed 8

Biking to High Altitudes 9

Vote "Yes" for the Skate Park 10

Interesting Animals

How to Teach Your Dog Basic Commands 11

The Ant and the Grasshopper 12

Max, the Seeing-Eye Puppy 13

The Dog and the Hare 14

Speedy Cheetahs 15

Building Character

Alaskan Rescue 16

A Violin for George 17

If Offended, Forgive 18

Stay in Bed, Adam 19

Set a Goal, Make It Happen 20

Timed Passage 21

Timed Passage 22

Word List 23

Fluency Practice

 Read the story to each other.

 Read the story on your own.

 Read the story to your partner again. Try to read the story even better.

 Questions? Ask your partner two questions about the story. Tell each other about the story you just read.

Timed Reading

1. When you do a timed reading with your partner, make sure that you have practiced your story and know all the words.

2. When you are ready, tell your partner to start the timer.

3. Read carefully, and your partner will stop you at 1 minute. When you stop, mark your place.

4. Count the total number of words you read.

5. In the back of your Student Book, write the number of words you read and color in the squares on your Fluency Chart.

6. Now switch with your partner.

Symbols on the Dollar Bill

The next time you have a minute and some cash, look closely at a dollar bill. Inspect the symbols on the bill because they tell a story. Some reflect the hopes and dreams of the founding leaders of the United States.

If you look closely at the dollar bill, you'll see the motto, "In God We Trust." On either side of the motto are two circles. The circle on the left holds a pyramid and an eye. The pyramid stands for strength and endurance. Notice that the pyramid is unfinished. The missing part may represent the early leaders' hope that our country would grow and improve. ⁽¹⁰⁶⁾ The "all-seeing eye" above the pyramid is an ancient symbol for God.

The circle on the right shows an eagle, which is the national bird. The eagle on the dollar holds an olive branch in one claw and arrows in the other. The olive branch and arrows represent peace and war.

Look closely at the banner in the eagle's beak. The words on it are written in Latin and mean "one nation from many people."

Above the eagle, you'll find 13 stars. They stand for the original 13 colonies. The shield in front of the eagle has 13 stripes. The white bar at the top of the shield, which seems to hold the stripes together, stands for Congress. ⁽²²⁵⁾

PASSAGE 2

SIGNS AND SYMBOLS

Too Many Red Things

Ashley and Jed were so bored in the car that they felt like screaming. They were on their way to visit Aunt Kathleen with their parents. They always had a terrific time with their aunt and cousins, but the drive to their house lasted six hours. Ashley already had played with her compass and read a book about geography, and Jed had read a whole book and drawn a picture.

"Mom, can you think of anything else for us to do?" Ashley moaned.

Mom inspected the map on her lap. "We're coming to a town called Applewood. I'll reward you with a dime for every red sign you spot."

As they pulled into town, Ashley called out, "There's a theater, and the letters on the front are red. (128) Do I get a dime for every letter?"

Mom laughed, "That's a lot of letters, but why not? The dimes should provide you with enough money to spend with your cousins."

Then, Jed called out, "There's a red stop sign, and the letters on that store's motto, 'Our Best to You,' are red."

As they rode along, they spotted so many red signs that they became bored with the game.

Finally, they pulled up in front of Aunt Kathleen's house. As Aunt Kathleen hurried out to greet them followed by two of her children, Ashley and Jed glanced at each other and started giggling. Everyone who came out of the house was wearing something red! (243)

SIGNS AND SYMBOLS

PASSAGE 3

A Visit to the Vietnam Memorial

Yesterday was a day I always will remember. My class took a field trip to the Vietnam Memorial in our nation's capital. The structure was built to honor soldiers who lost their lives in the Vietnam War. As we walked toward it, we must have looked like soldiers ourselves. We wore the school uniform, which includes navy shorts and light blue T-shirts. The front of the shirts shows the school's motto, "Hope for the Future."

The memorial is a long black wall with the names of more than 50,000 people on it. Each name is a person who died in the war or has never been found. The wall starts off low and grows in height as you walk along. All my friends grew quiet and serious as we passed name after name after name. When we reached the center of the wall, we turned a corner and kept walking past more names. I saw that some people had left notes and flowers for their loved ones. Others were making rubbings of names along the wall.

The wall helps us remember the military people and reflects the lives they sacrificed. When we left the wall, I thought of the motto on my shirt. I decided that my hope for the future is freedom for all people.

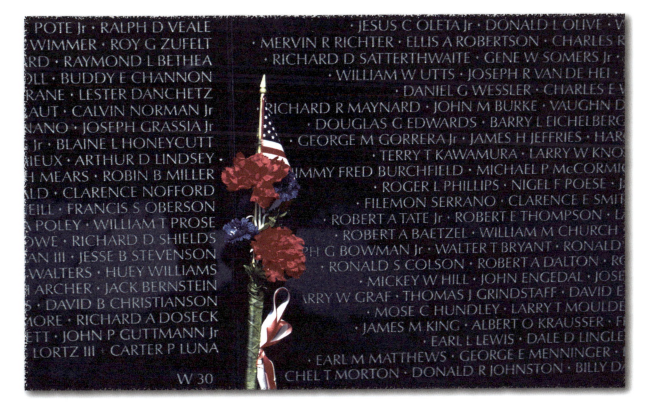

Looking at Maps

People have used maps that include pictures of places since early times. Some maps show small places such as a school, while others show large places, such as a continent. Early maps were simple drawings. However, today's maps are very complex. In fact, some maps are even made from photographs taken by satellites.

There are many different types of maps. Some may show the natural geography of a place. Others may show roads and highways or the borders of a state or country. Some maps even provide information about events in history.

The first thing to look for when you study a map is its title. The title tells you what area the map shows. (115)

Next, take a look at the map key. It shows symbols that are used on the map, and it explains what the symbols stand for. Symbols on maps stand for things from airports to state capitals.

One of the most important symbols on a map is the compass rose. The compass rose shows the cardinal directions—north, south, east, and west as well as northeast, southeast, southwest, and northwest.

Before you begin using a map, you should inspect the map scale. This tool gives you the measurements you need to figure out real distances. For example, an inch may represent hundreds of miles on a map of Africa but only a few yards on a map of your school. (234)

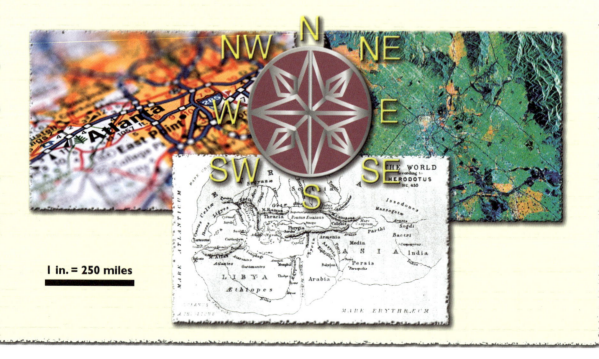

SIGNS AND SYMBOLS

PASSAGE 5

The Bald Eagle

You probably know that the bald eagle is our national symbol. But did you know that it took the country's founding leaders six years to choose an animal to represent our nation? They wanted to think of a symbol that would bring honor to the new nation. Many had their own ideas about what animal that would be. In fact, Ben Franklin fought long and hard in favor of the wild turkey.

The bald eagle finally was selected as the national symbol in 1782. The leaders felt that the eagle would reflect all that the nation and its people stood for. (101) They believed that the eagle stood for strength and courage. Most important, the eagle stood for freedom.

Bald eagles are large and powerful birds. They can weigh up to 14 pounds, and when flying, their wings can stretch more than 8 feet. Bald eagles mate for life and build their nests in the tops of tall trees. Each year, they add more twigs to the nests. Over time, a nest can grow to be 10 feet long, about the length of a small car, and weigh as much as a ton. (192)

5

PASSAGE 1

EXCITING GAMES

The Winter Watch
Your source for winter recreational events

January   Issue 15 • Volume 36   Extreme Fun Section

Family from Lee County Enjoys New Sport

Story by I.C. Conditions
Freelance writer for the North Pole Gazette

For the last two years, Jim and Susan Smith and their son George have enjoyed a new sport. They race snowmobiles in a winter sport called snowcross. Snowcross is similar to another extreme sport—motocross. In both sports, riders combine exciting jumps with difficult courses.

"Snowcross has been featured in the Winter X Games on TV," says Jim. "In fact, that's how we got interested in it. We were watching TV when George, who was 10, asked if he could try the sport. Susan and I thought it would be a way for the family to spend time together doing something we enjoy. We agreed with George."

The Smith family races every weekend when the weather cooperates. They even travel from state to state to compete. Last year, Susan competed in a national event held in Vermont. (137) "I didn't win, but I loved watching the graceful moves of the other athletes," she said.

Even though George is the youngest, he has been the most successful in snowcross events. In fact, he is second in his class so far this season. "At first, snowcross scared me," he says. "I was especially frightened at the beginning of each race. That's when all the snowmobiles are crammed together. I've gotten used to it though."

Called "sleds," the snowmobiles can reach speeds of 90 miles per hour. To protect themselves, the athletes wear helmets, special boots, and knee guards. Most people also wear chest guards.

To stay in good physical shape, the Smiths stay active year round. During the summers, they enjoy water skiing and hiking. (262)

6

EXCITING GAMES

Climbing Walls of Rock

Larry loved watching extreme sports on television and reading about them in the newspaper. Then one day, he decided to try one of these sports himself. He was attracted to rock climbing. It involves climbing the flat faces of cliffs. He soon learned that a course on beginning rock climbing was offered at his high school.

He discovered that rock climbing requires a lot of strength. "My arms were pretty strong, so I thought it would be easy," he says, "but I soon found that you need to have very strong legs and feet too. I also had to learn to stay focused so I wouldn't fall. At one point, I almost gave up the sport, but I was determined to stay with it. There's nothing like the feeling of triumph I have when I've completed a climb." (138)

Rock climbing is safer than some extreme sports. One reason for this is because of the new safety designs for climbing equipment. Another reason is that trained teachers usually teach the courses. Most courses are taught indoors. This means that each situation can be carefully controlled, and students can be closely watched.

"About 80 percent of all climbers learn to climb indoors," says Anne Yates, a rock-climbing teacher. "Of course, when a climber moves outdoors, there can be surprises," she says. "It's very easy to go too high." Smith thinks that rock climbing is one of the most exciting sports of all. "Anyone can do it," she adds, "as long as the person is in good physical shape before beginning." (259)

If at First You Don't Succeed

"Ethan, are you hurt?" Mom asked, carrying a load of wash to the garage.

"Nope, I'm all right," Ethan answered, brushing off his pants and picking up his skateboard. "I just can't seem to get the hang of doing this new trick. I've already wiped out four times."

As his mother disappeared into the garage, Ethan checked the nuts and bolts on his skateboard. "Maybe there's a loose screw or something," he thought. Seeing that they were tight, he made a deal with himself. "I'll try the trick one more time. If I nail it, I'll keep skating, but if I wipe out, I'll go do my homework and try again later." ⑫

Ethan tightened the chinstrap on his helmet, pulled his elbow pads into place, and took a deep breath. He was ready to try another ollie, or jump, with his board. He really wanted to learn the trick before the exhibition because he had signed up to perform in the junior division. As Ethan pushed off, he noticed his classmate Anna coming out of the house next door. Then, his mother walked out of the garage.

With his board picking up speed, Ethan crouched down and tried to remember the proper method for doing an ollie. Then, he quickly snapped the tail and jumped up, with the board lifting gracefully into the air.

When he landed, his mother and Anna cheered his successful attempt.

"I guess I just needed an audience," Ethan smiled, picking up his board. ㉔⑧

EXCITING GAMES

PASSAGE 4

Biking to High Altitudes

You've probably ridden a bike across flat land, but did you know that there's a sport called flatlanding? This sport involves riding in flat places, but with a "bag full of tricks." The tricks have names, such as the dump truck and the elephant glide.

The tricks in flatlanding aren't for the faint of heart. They're for people who love physical challenges. To perform most of the stunts, riders have only a part of their bodies on the bike. Their arms and legs are swinging wildly in the air. So are their bikes for that matter. (96) The tricks can be difficult to learn, but they're awesome to watch.

Another bike riding sport is called dirt jumping. This sport, not surprisingly, involves dirt—and a lot of it. Riders go over jumps and ramps made of dirt, hoping to fly higher than their rivals. One well-known dirt riding spot is shaped like a huge bowl. Located in Riverside, California, it has attracted many famous dirt jumpers.

Like flatlanders, dirt jumpers like to do stunts. If you can imagine yourself flying up, up, and up, and then doing a graceful backflip with your bike, you'd probably love dirt bike sports. (199)

9

Vote "Yes" for the Skate Park

Next week, the people of our city will vote whether we should build a skate park near the community center. Vote "Yes" for this fantastic idea! There are more than 16 million skateboarders in the United States today. Some of those skaters live here. Yet, these athletes do not have a place to enjoy their sport because city laws do not allow skating in public places. We all know that skaters can be a danger to people who are on foot. So why not give them a place of their own?

Some people in this community look down on skateboarding. They are determined to stop the building of the park. These people should know that skating has become a popular sport. ⑫¹ Skateboarding is even one of the sports featured at the Summer X Games.

In some places, people object to the noise that the parks bring to neighborhoods. In our town, this would not be a problem. The community center is located in a busy part of the city, one that already is noisy.

Ten years ago, there were only a few skate parks in the nation. Today, there are more than a thousand. In most of these places, the parks have been quite successful. Let's add another skate park to the growing list. A park will give our teens something to do and a safe place in which to do it. Vote "Yes," and both our skaters and our city will triumph! ㉴³

How to Teach Your Dog Basic Commands

If you have a dog that doesn't obey you, you'll probably agree that it's time for a change. You'll certainly be happier with a well-behaved dog, and your dog will be happier too.

If you have a puppy, it will be ready for its first training sessions when it's about 12 weeks old. Older dogs can be trained. Just remember that their training may take a little longer. Practice the following commands for about 10 minutes twice a day, then slowly increase the length of the sessions as necessary.

Teaching Fido to Come to You

Begin teaching your dog to approach you by standing nearby with a treat. Say the dog's name, and wait for it to notice the treat. When your dog begins walking toward you, clearly say, "Come." When it reaches your side, offer the treat with praise for what a marvelous animal it is. (148)

Do this for your dog's first few efforts, then gradually start saying, "Come," before your dog begins walking toward you.

Teaching Rover to Sit

Teach your dog to sit by standing to the side with a treat while calling its name. When your dog comes toward you, slowly raise the treat in the air. This will force it to sit down while following the treat. Then say, "Sit," in a clear voice and kindly offer the treat.

If your dog won't sit when you hold up the food, gently hold the collar in one hand. Then, guide it into a sitting position while firmly saying, "Sit." Reward your dog with the treat and a lot of praise. Soon your dog will obey the verbal command alone. Continue to raise your hand over the dog's head to teach this signal too. (288)

The Ant and the Grasshopper

"Ah, what a marvelous morning!" Grasshopper chirped contentedly. "It's a great time for singing and playing." He leaned back to rest against a blade of grass and began humming.

About that time, Ant passed by, dragging with great effort a huge crumb of bread that he had found along the road.

"Greetings, Ant," said Grasshopper. "Why not join me in singing and playing instead of working so hard?" he asked.

Ant looked at Grasshopper with pity and replied, "I'm helping set aside food for the winter, and I have some good advice for you. You should do the same."

"Who cares about winter?" asked Grasshopper, bending over to take a bite of a tender shoot of ivy. ⑪⑦

"There's plenty of food now," he said, licking his lips.

"Yes," answered Ant, "it's a wonderful opportunity, and you should take advantage of it."

Ant continued to toil every day throughout the summer and fall, dragging food bit by bit to his home. Slowly, the amount of food he had stored increased, and he finally stopped to relax.

Weeks later, when the ground was covered in snow and icicles dripped from trees, Ant was comfortable and warm in his home. Each day, he brought out a bit of food to enjoy. A few feet away, Grasshopper shivered in the cold. Hungry and miserable, Grasshopper realized that Ant had been right. It is best to prepare for times of need. ㉛⑥

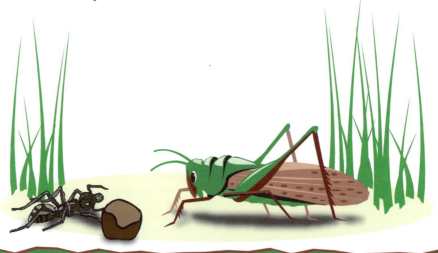

INTERESTING ANIMALS

PASSAGE 3

Max, the Seeing-Eye Puppy

"Come, Max," Lisa says to her new puppy. Max bounds up to her and licks her face. While she strokes her puppy, Lisa explains that Max has been selected to be a seeing-eye dog for a blind person. Max is a black lab, a breed known for being gentle and intelligent.

She says that Max will leave her home after a year to receive special training at a school for guide dogs. He'll learn to help a blind person walk safely on city sidewalks and move through crowded malls. He'll even learn to keep this new friend out of danger.

Lisa's job is to teach Max social skills and good manners before he receives his formal training. At the tender age of 6 months, he still has a lot to learn. (132) "It is hard work," Lisa explains. "A new puppy is like a baby. He didn't know how to do anything when I first got him, but with time, his skills have increased a lot." Like a proud parent, Lisa continues, "Max mastered a huge hurdle last week when he stayed calm in a crowd of people at my school's soccer game."

Lisa has learned a lot about training puppies at the puppy club meetings she and Max attend every week. She has taught Max to lie by her left side when she eats and to sleep by her bed. Max also has learned never to climb on furniture or to beg for table scraps.

"I'll really miss Max when he leaves," Lisa says. "But, my parents have enjoyed this experience as much as I have, so we plan to raise another puppy soon." (275)

13

The Dog and the Hare

Hare was hopping along the road one day and enjoying the blue sky, the white feathery clouds, and the warm sun. He spotted Dog lying in the shade of an enormous maple tree, so he cheerfully approached him. "Delightful morning, Dog!" said Hare. "Isn't this a marvelous day?"

Dog leapt to his feet, his tail wagging so rapidly his whole body swayed to and fro. With a gleeful smile, he replied excitedly, "Hello there, Hare, let's play tag. You chase me first."

Grinning at the thought of an enchanting morning playing with Dog, Hare agreed. Dog took off and hurried across the meadow, zigging and zagging through the wildflowers with Hare close behind.

After a few minutes, Hare caught Dog and tagged him. "Now, it's my turn—catch me if you can!" Hare hollered, racing toward a grove of trees. (140) Dog was enjoying the game so much that he began barking, which made Hare nervous and caused him to increase his speed.

Dog scampered faster and faster until finally he caught Hare. He was having so much fun that he playfully opened his mouth, placed it around Hare's fluffy tail, and pushed Hare to the ground. The two animals tumbled down a hillside—Hare's heart pounding swiftly in his chest. "This is really terrifying," thought Hare. "I don't like it when Dog plays so rough because it makes me insecure."

At the bottom of the hill, Hare shook himself free from Dog's grip and glared at his friend angrily. He began scampering away, saying over his shoulder, "No more of this game, Dog. I've told you before not to play so rough, and I have some advice for you. Say you are sorry, and promise you won't push me down. I won't play with you again until I'm certain I can trust you." With that, Hare hastily hopped down the road toward home. (313)

Speedy Cheetahs

Slowly count to four—one . . . two . . . three . . . four. That's not a very long time, is it? But 4 seconds is all the time it takes for a cheetah to move from a standstill to a run at more than 60 miles an hour.

Cheetahs, the fastest of all land animals, have bodies built like running machines. Their large hearts pump extra blood, and their extra-wide nostrils take in a lot of air. Their long legs help them cover more than 20 feet with each stride, while their long tails balance and guide them. They even have grooved footpads and sturdy claws that help them grip the ground as they run.

Running 60 miles an hour takes a lot of energy, so cheetahs tire easily. Because of this, they cannot run long distances. Instead, they use quick bursts of speed to catch prey such as zebras, antelopes, and hares. Cheetahs run best when they move in a straight line, so an animal that makes twists and turns has an advantage.

Like most big cats, cheetahs are an endangered species. Many live in the southern part of Africa near private ranching land. Some ranchers view them as pests, and thousands of cheetahs have been killed during the last decade.

Efforts now are being made to protect and save these beautiful creatures. Perhaps one day you will have an opportunity to see these speedy animals in the wild.

Alaskan Rescue

Several years ago, a person crashed a snowmobile into a tree near Aniak, Alaska. Within minutes, rescue workers were on their way to care for the injured driver. At the scene, the workers took a glimpse of the injured man and proceeded to save his life.

Called the Dragon Slayers, this group is the only rescue team in this wilderness area of Alaska. Yet the team isn't like most rescue groups. It is made up of teenagers.

The Dragon Slayers serve people from 14 small villages. They are on call around the clock. They've rescued people from fires, accidents, and even a plane crash. They respond to about 400 calls a year—more than one call on most days! They often have to leave school to do the job. ⁽¹²⁹⁾

The Dragon Slayers must be well trained. Each person receives 200 hours of medical and safety training.

The group was started by a man named Pete Brown. More than a decade ago, Brown's son was injured in an accident. He had to wait a long time for help to arrive. Brown decided that his region needed its own emergency service. He began training adults to do the work, and soon, teenagers began to join. As time passed, the adults dropped out because they couldn't spend the time required for the job.

Several years ago, the Dragon Slayers received an award. They were chosen as the best ambulance service in Alaska. Some of the members chuckle at the thought of this achievement. "We usually just jump in the nearest pickup truck and take off," one of them says. ⁽²⁶⁶⁾

Building Character

PASSAGE 2

A Violin for George

George sat up in bed and looked out the window. "Another beautiful day," he said smiling. Swinging his legs over the side of his bed, he picked up his imaginary violin and adjusted it on his shoulder. Then, he pretended to play a song while humming its melody. Just as the song ended, his mother called him for breakfast.

George rushed downstairs and sat down at the kitchen table. Handing him a plate and a newspaper, his mother said, "Take a look at this, George." She pointed to an ad for Hal's Music Store. George took a glimpse at the ad, and his eyes grew larger. The ad said that all of the used violins in Hal's would be on sale for four weeks. George, who had been taking violin lessons for the last two years, had been using the violin at school to practice. (145)

Even though he tried to have patience, he couldn't wait to have a violin of his very own.

George had saved some money from baby-sitting jobs, and his generous parents had offered to match every dollar he made. He figured he needed about $30 more to buy one of Hal's violins. But how could he make that much money before the sale ended?

George remembered that two of his neighbors were going out of town soon. "Mom, do you think the McCoys and the Smiths would hire me to take care of their houses while they're gone? I could mow their lawns, bring in their newspapers, and water their plants. Come to think of it, I even could feed Scrappy, the Smiths' cat. What do you think?"

"I think it's a wonderful idea," his mom answered, smiling.

That is just what George did. (289)

If Offended, Forgive

An ancient proverb says, "If you offend, ask for a pardon; if offended, forgive." The world would be a kinder and more generous place if everyone acted on this idea.

Not long ago, Laura Ford put the idea into practice. A young man's car ran into the side of her car while she was driving. Ford's two children were in the back seat, and one of them was injured slightly.

When the accident occurred, the driver of the other car sped away. Ford wrote down the license plate number. Later, the police called her to say that they had found the person who had run into her. He was only 16 years old.

Ford asked to meet the young man at the police station. "I found a very frightened teenager named Jim," she said. "He confessed that he had made a terrible mistake and that he regretted his actions. At that moment, I made a conscious decision. I forgave him rather than pressing charges."

Ford's act of forgiveness meant that Jim could keep his new driver's license. It also meant that he could continue to help his mother, who was ill, with her errands. He later said that he learned a lot from this experience. The biggest lesson was that forgiveness is a powerful act.

Today, Jim gives talks in public schools. He uses humor to tell students the story about his accident and what he learned from it. He encourages them to behave with honor, never to cheat another person, and to respect and have patience with others and themselves. He also reminds them to forgive those who have offended them.

BUILDING CHARACTER

PASSAGE 4

Stay in Bed, Adam

Adam plumped up his pillow and stared at the clock by his bed. He had sprained his ankle, and his doctor said he had to stay off his feet for a while. He normally would volunteer at the homeless shelter at this time, and he hated to miss it.

"I'd better do something, or I'll go crazy," he thought, reaching for a pad of paper and some colorful pens. He proceeded to sketch the scene outside his window.

When his father walked in a few minutes later, Adam's face broke into a smile. "Say, Dad, what do mice have for breakfast?" he teased. Without waiting for his father to respond, he finished, "Mice Crispies!" (114)

Laughing aloud, his father handed him an apple for a snack. "Let me know if you need anything else, goofy kid," he said.

Adam had just finished the apple when his sister came in. "It must be boring having to stay in bed all day," she said.

"It's not so bad," Adam replied, handing her the picture he had drawn. "Here, I drew this for you."

A little later, Adam decided to write a letter to his cousin Frank. He told Frank all about his accident and added a few jokes. When he was addressing the envelope, his mother walked in and kindly asked him how he was doing.

"I feel completely useless lying here," Adam admitted.

His mother thought for a minute. "Well, let's see. You've made your sister happy by drawing her a picture, you've made your father laugh by telling him a joke, and you've written your cousin a letter. I'd say you've been quite generous. Your achievement this afternoon has been making others happy." (282)

19

Set a Goal, Make It Happen

Have you ever wanted to try something new but didn't know how to get started? Perhaps you wanted to learn to speak a new language or to improve your skills in a sport. Setting goals is one way you can achieve such dreams. Having a goal can give your life direction. It can give you a glimpse into your own future. Yet, many people find it difficult to set goals and make them happen.

How to Make a Plan

The first step in setting goals is to define what you want to do. Your definition should identify a specific action that is within your reach. It also should include the date by which you want to achieve the goal. For example, you might write, "I would like to be able to swim across the pool by the end of the summer," instead of, "I would like to be an Olympic swimmer when I grow up." Put your list of goals in a place that you see every day. Then, proceed to make your dreams become reality.

How to Make It Happen

The next step is to identify several smaller steps that will lead to your goal. Imagine that your goal is to make and serve your dad a good dessert on Father's Day. You would need to break this goal into smaller steps that might include finding a recipe for chocolate cake, buying the things to make it, and baking the cake before Father's Day.

Something to Think About

Before you begin working toward your goal, imagine yourself doing each step with great ease and skill. Then, start to work to bring this imaginary goal to life. You will be amazed at your achievements.

Are You a Good Friend?

The writer Ralph Waldo Emerson once said, "The only way to have a friend is to be one." Although this idea is easy to understand, it is not always easy to carry out. Let's face it, sometimes it's hard to be a good friend. Read the following checklist and see how many of these characteristics of a good friend describe you.

I Show Respect for My Friends.

Showing respect is a great way to be a loyal friend. That means that you do not tease your friend with unkind comments or talk about the person behind his or her back. It also means that you do not try to convince your friend to do something that he or she does not want to do. (124)

I Listen to My Friends' Thoughts and Ideas.

As you know, close friends talk about everything from sports and music to things that are bothering them. When you talk to a friend, be a good listener by paying careful attention to your friend's words and waiting for your turn to speak.

I Invite My Friends to Go Places and Do Things with Me.

Do you ever feel sorry for yourself because you have not been invited somewhere by a friend? The solution to this problem is simple—pick up the phone and call your friend. Invite your friend to come to your house, to go to a movie, or to take a walk.

I Have Fun with My Friends.

Having fun with your friends is one of the best ways to build a friendship, and it's also very good for you. Studies have shown that laughing and being with friends are two important ways to stay healthy. (281)

Not Now, Ralph!

"Mike, catch this," whispered Ralph, twirling a bright green Frisbee on his finger. Their teacher, Ms. Brown, had just stepped outside the classroom to talk to the principal. She had told the class to write their answers to the questions about the Lewis and Clark expedition.

Mike turned to look at Ralph, who sat seven rows behind him. He mouthed the words, "Not now," and turned back to his work. He tried to think of an original answer to the first question.

Wanting to convince his friend to play, Ralph whispered even more urgently, "Come on, Mike, catch it!"

Mike, whose concentration now was broken, thought, "Maybe if I just throw the Frisbee to Ralph one time, he'll let me work." He turned and signaled to Ralph that he was ready to play. (133)

Ralph smiled and with a mighty effort, sent the Frisbee spiraling over the heads of several classmates toward Mike's desk.

The Frisbee glided straight toward Mike, but then took a turn to the left and sailed into the lamp on Ms. Brown's desk, knocking it over.

As the lamp tumbled over, Ms. Brown opened the door. When she saw what had happened, she walked to her desk with an alarmed expression and picked up the lamp. Mike breathed a sigh of relief to see that it wasn't broken.

"Who did this?" she asked sharply, setting the lamp back in its place.

Ralph quickly jumped to his feet and confessed, "I did, Ms. Brown." From the corner of his eye, Mike saw Ralph wave his hand to signal Mike to stay seated.

Smiling at his loyal friend, Mike slowly stood up and said, "I'm afraid it was my fault too." (282)

Word List

provide	determined
reflect	triumph
military	exhibition
sacrificed	marvelous
weigh	increase
graceful	advice